THE REAL HIPHOP